My Name Is Harry Worth

Roy Baines

The story of one of Britain's best loved comedians

To Dad – Thank you for teaching me not just to laugh,
but the reasons behind it.

ISBN 9780955185403

Thanks go to Harry's daughter Jobyna, whose invaluable help made this book possible.
The author would also like to thank the following for providing material for the book.

John Ammonds, Michael Grade CBE, William G. Stewart, Debbie Cumming, Jimmy Cricket,
Norman Lovett, A J Marriot, Glenn Mitchell, TV Times, Woman's Own,
Manchester City Council, Starbucks.

Whilst every effort has been made to trace and acknowledge all copyright holders,
I would like to apologise should there have been any errors or omissions.

**Published by
MRA Publishing
Brooke House
Stilton
Peterborough
PE7 3XG**

Foreword by John Ammonds

I first met Harry Worth in the 1950's when I booked him to do his stand-up act in a show in Manchester where I was working as a BBC radio producer. His rather nervous, self deprecating style had caught my attention when he was compering an ITV program coming from London. When he was on my show, he finished the act with something which illustrates his individual quality "I would very much like to do some more, but I don't <u>know</u> anymore!"

The next time we met was a year or so later in 1959. I was still in Manchester, but was now working in TV. Harry was appearing in a revue type show at the opera House called "Large As Life" starring Harry Secombe, which had just completed a very successful nine months run at the London Palladium. Harry was quite taken aback when I saw him in his dressing room and offered him the starring role in his own TV situation comedy! I explained that, although this pilot programme was only being transmitted on BBC North and at 10.30 at night! We hoped that, when the recording was sent to London and seen by the Entertainment Dept. there, they would like it and offer us a series on the Network.

Before I had approached Harry, my boss had asked me to fill a 30-minute space, if possible a show, which could be developed into a series. The following day, I suggested Harry Worth, and said I was confident that, with his individual brand of comedy, we had a good chance of success. Fortunately, my Head of Department agreed!!

The pilot was entitled The Dithering Detective and, although Harry and a very good cast did well, I have to say that the reaction of the smallish audience (remember it was 10.30pm) was not over the moon!! It took a long while to get the script together. In fact, at one point Harry said "John, it's taken us 2 months to do this one show. What happens if London gives us a series of 6? We dare not be successful." In the event, we <u>were</u> successful and got the series, although London were very surprised that, in the first show, Harry did not appear as an inefficient detective but in a new situation in his auntie's house but still confusing everybody with whom he came into contact! We explained

John Ammonds

that we all thought it would be difficult to sustain the detective idea for a series. Over 60 more shows were done in Manchester in a very small studio, a converted church long since pulled down. Once the sets were in, the size of the audience was limited to 70 – the London studios can hold 350!!

Roy Baines has written in this book about the various writers who worked on Here's Harry. Many thanks are due to them and to the many other people who worked so hard to make Harry such a well-known character throughout the country, playing to audiences of 14 million and above.

I shall remember those years of producing the show with affection. Yes, we had difficulties common to most comedy programmes, rewrites and still more rewrites, but the results made it all worthwhile and this book will bring back memories of a hard working true professional who was also a very nice man.

John Ammonds
2005

Introduction

Auntie, Tiddles, 52 Acacia Avenue, trilby hat & glasses. All things that instantly bring to mind one of Britain's best-loved comedians of the classic era of comedy – Harry Worth.

My first memories of Harry were of Sunday nights, being allowed to stay up to watch his antics on TV and remembering how much my father enjoyed him as well, and, as today, the playground talk may be of the latest comedy craze – Peter Kaye or League of Gentlemen etc, it was talk of Harry in those days. Finding a corner wall in the playground to imitate Harry's trademark 'arm & leg' routine, imitating his mannerisms, even answering the teacher in his style. All good clean harmless fun with not a hint of violence, disrespect or malice.

The impressionists of the time also had a field day, Mike Yarwood, Peter Goodwright, Bobby Bennett all eager to copy his style.

While writing this book I have confirmed what most people must have thought about Harry. He was a warm, caring but very private person, loved by his millions of fans and highly respected in showbusiness circles. He loved and adored his family and treasured the times he spent with them. I was not fortunate enough to have met him but speaking to his family, friends and fellow artiste's, I feel that I did. Thank you Harry for the legacy you have left behind, your place in showbusiness history is assured.

Roy Baines

Stone Road, Tankersley. Just yards from the pit where Harry worked. It was the house with the pram outside.

Harry at school, back row 4th from right.

My Name Is Harry Worth

Roy Baines

On November 20th 1917 at 47 Fitzwilliam Street, Hoyland Common, Near Barnsley the world was introduced to Harry Bourlon Illingsworth. Little did his parents know then that any confusion, mayhem or disruption he may have caused entering this world would pale in to insignificance to that which was to follow in later years.

The house in Fitzwilliam Street, which is still there today, was a typical terraced house with an outside loo but was the family home of Charles Henry Illingsworth & Alice Jane Illingsworth (nee Crick) and their 11 children, Harry being the 11th.

Irene, Died 18/12/1909 aged 12mths – Flu

Eveline, Died 7/12/1909 aged 2yrs 6mths – Flu

Lloyd George, Died 9/6/1914 aged 14yrs 3mths – Meningitis

Irving, Died 1918 aged 20yrs – Killed in action

Stanley (1), Born 1901 – Died as a baby

Stanley (2), Died 1982 aged 80

Ivy, Had 7 children – (Irvin, Cynthia, Leslie, Phyllis, Kenneth, Ron & Dorothy)

Harold, Died 1982 aged 77

Laurence, Died aged 51 – Was a guard at Buckingham Palace

Dora, no records of her traceable.

Harry's father Charles, died in a pit accident at the age of 47, six months after Harry was born. In those days help was virtually non-existent and Alice was

A return visit to the mine

forced into taking in washing to help make ends meet. She also made scones, which Harry would sell around the village. When Harry was 11 they moved to 107 Stone Road, Tankersley which was only about 100yds from the pit where he started working 3 years later. The house and mine has long since gone and a new housing development stands where it once was.

Harry's flair for showbusiness became evident when, armed with a Magic Lantern, he used to put on shows in his shed, charging other children to watch. Whilst at school a visiting ventriloquist gave a show and Harry was immediately hooked. He borrowed a book from the library, which he vigorously studied and so convincing him that he could do it as well. His first dummy Clarence was borrowed from a girl in the village but he later bought 2 vent dolls, one for 3/11d (19p) at a Blackpool novelty stall and another for 55/- (£2.75) from Gamages in 1935, which he paid back at 10/-(50p) a month.

At the age of 14 Harry left school and, with the check number of 166 went to work down the Pilley Mine loading the cage at the bottom of the shaft, later on moving to the Wharncliffe Silkstone pit. He once said *"I lived in a world of my own most of the time. As I worked at the coalface, I'd be there at the Palladium doing my act – to myself, if there was no one else around to listen. I did some of my best work down number four pit. Marvellous receptions I got and my press – you'd never believe how good it was!"*

Whilst down the pit he was constantly practising his voice throwing skills. The practising paid off when he won an amateur concert at the Alhambra Theatre, Barnsley as a Ventriloquist, the prize being a radiogram, but it wasn't electric, something that he had wanted so much, so he sold it and bought a radio with a liquid battery. He was a member of the Village Cycle Club and they once planned to cycle to London. When it came to the day he was the only one that turned up so he decided to do it on his own. He cycled from Yorkshire to Suffolk and then to London (first time he had visited the city) then on to Bournemouth and back home to Yorkshire. A trip which, at the age of 16, took him 2 weeks to complete.

In Service.

1st from left 2nd row. And who's that right at the front?

"It goes here somewhere!!"

Concert Party Antics

Although it was tradition to work 'down't pit' the attraction of the footlights was beckoning so in 1938 he became a full time entertainer and worked the local Working Men's Clubs. He belonged to both the Pilley Drama Group & the Tankersley Players appearing in several local productions but, although the roar of the crowd and the bright lights were miles away, this was soon to change. The next year saw him entering the Royal Air Force as T.A.C (Elec.) Aircraftsman Second Class, Illingsworth H and became an aircraft fitter stationed at RAF Halton regularly appearing in camp concerts. His NCO was reported as saying "As a fitter, you are a very good ventriloquist". It was initially a problem joining up as mining was deemed a reserve occupation. Eventually the rules were relaxed and Harry was able to enter the RAF. After 3 weeks mining was once again made a reserved occupation because so many had joined up there was a shortage of workers in the pits so Harry just managed to get in. He had said that he was one of the happiest men to ever enter the camp because he could see daylight all day long, a vast improvement on his days in the mines. Also stationed there was a young WAAF Kay Flynn but despite her also being a fitter they never actually met whilst at Halton – but their paths were to cross in later years.

He served in Egypt, Palestine & Burma and while he was in Burma there was a call went out for anyone interested in entertaining to go down to Delhi for an audition. Harry did not hesitate and was soon making his way there and, within 10 days, he was in *The Gang Show* show. He remembered that nothing that happened to him afterwards - the appearing at the Palladium, the spot in the Royal Command Performance, the television series - had ever thrilled him as much as being picked for that show.

Once the war was over Harry never really believed he would be an entertainer. His favourite comedians of that time were Robb Wilton, Jimmy James and Albert Modley. He once said: - *"I dreamed about being an entertainer, but that was all. I never thought that such luxuries as going on the stage and visiting places with strange-sounding names, like Burnley & Huddersfield, would ever come my way. But they did!"*

One of his earliest engagements after the war was at West Cliff Gardens, Clacton where he was billed as The Versatile Vent. He spent long days trudging round theatrical agents offices with other ex-service entertainers such as Eric Sykes, Harry Secombe, Peter

KAY FLYNN

Sellers, Morecambe & Wise etc. Kay persuaded him to write for an audition at the Windmill theatre in London. When he arrived he found he was one of over 40 waiting to audition. Impresario Vivian Van Damm never laughed once throughout his act but, much to Harry's surprise, he was booked. He worked with Eric & Ernie at the Windmill theatre in 1948- they were paid off after one week, because Van Damm didn't care much for double acts, only to go on to become one of the greatest comedy double acts of all time. Harry remained good friends with both Ernie Wise & Harry Secombe, sharing the same interest in boating with Ernie Wise. Also on the same bill as Harry at the Windmill was Tony Hancock, accompanied by pianist Derek Scott.

We mentioned earlier about a young WAFF Kay Flynn who was also stationed at RAF Halton. In 1946 Harry landed a job in Pantomime – Babes in the Wood at the Theatre Royal Lincoln. Kay was principal girl and was billed higher than Harry. It was very soon evident to everyone in the show that they were made for each other as they were never apart for the entire run. Kay had decided by now that Harry was the person for her and could not wait for him to ask her for her hand in marriage. When the show ended its run and it was time for goodbyes Harry went over to Kay, who thought 'this is it', but he simply said 'Cheerio Kay'. Kay was so upset that she cried herself to sleep that night. Next morning, still feeling devastated she arrived at the station for her train back to Wales. As the train was about to pull out of the station Harry was seen running down the platform calling Kay's name. He flung his arms around her and told her how much he loved her and that he wanted to marry her. They were married at a Registry Office in Cardiff on 4th October 1947, 9 months after meeting. Being just after the war money was very tight and the only other people present at the wedding were Kay's mother & two brothers, Frank & Tom. Kay started off in a trio with her brothers, Kay sung and Tom & Frank played musical instruments. Harry & Kay even went to the registry office by bus stopping of on the way for Harry to buy a ring and a pair of stockings for Kay. Harry could not afford to buy Kay a wedding ring so they used a curtain ring. The wedding night was spent on stage in a theatre near Cardiff. Harry promised Kay that he would buy her a proper one when he could afford it but, although he bought her many rings over the years, the wedding ring was never replaced and Kay wore it right up until the day she died.

Oliver Hardy's 62nd birthday celebrated onstage at Portsmouth. Harry can be seen in between Ollie & Stan.

The 1958 show which was to become a turning point in Harry's career

Their first home together was a flat in London at 157 Lynton Road W3. It was while living there that Harry's first TV show, The Dithering Detective, was broadcast. Kay had to watch it in a neighbours flat because they didn't have a TV.

Harry worked hard touring with his vent act billed as Harry Worth 'A Figure of Speech'. He had by now shortened the name Illingsworth to Worth. This was to enable him to be in bigger letters on billboards & posters and, when he finally became top of the bill, it was an asset.

In 1951 Kay fell pregnant and in May 1952 gave birth to their only child Jobyna. Harry worshipped Jo; she was his darling from the moment she was born. They decided that it was not right to travel all round the country with a young child so from then on Kay retired from showbusiness and concentrated on a harder career, that of bringing up a young daughter. Jo eventually went to boarding school at the age of 11, which was also a drama school. It was thought that, with Harry being an actor and Kay being a singer, if anything was to emerge it would, but in Jo's own words – there was nothing there to emerge.

Jo, who has been married and divorced and now happily remarried to Mike, has two children Dane & Emma. Harry idolised the grandchildren and was often seen doing somersaults down the garden for them. Kay used to tease him that his order of importance went First – Work, Second – Jo, Third – the Grandchildren, Fourth - Ingrid Bergman & Deanna Durbin and somewhere down the bottom of the list – Kay.

Harry continued to work with his vent act, Clarence & Fotheringay and in 1952/53 toured with Laurel & Hardy. It was during this tour that Ollie celebrated his 62nd birthday with an after show party onstage at Portsmouth. It was Oliver Hardy who saw the comedy potential in Harry and advised him to stop working with the dummies and to concentrate on a solo act. He eventually did while working with Harry Secombe and Eric Sykes in *Large as Life* at the London Palladium. He had been offered the part as a stand in for Terry Thomas who could not make the first house due to filming commitments. The first time he tried it he was so nervous without the dolls to hide behind that his dithering hesitant style, later to become his trademark, was born. He even started singing and tap dancing and normally finished his act with a cartwheel.

And as it was then.

The famous window in St Annes Square as it is today.
(Courtesy of Starbucks Ltd)

He received good reviews about the show, which gave him his big break. He never looked back from that point on. Ollie's advice had paid off but, when top of the bill in later years, he still introduced Clarence & Fotheringay.

After its run at the Palladium, *Large as Life* moved to the Opera House in Manchester. This is where Harry met TV producer John Ammonds, later to become responsible for producing & directing some of the greatest sketches in The Morecambe & Wise Shows and a meeting which was to place him firmly on the road to becoming a household name. Ammonds had been given the task of filling a half-hour slot on TV and was keen on doing so with a comedy. He had used Harry before in a variety show and thought that there was potential in his talent for a comedy show. Head of Programmes at the BBC at that time was Thurston Holland who, with John Ammonds, went to see Harry in Large as Life and agreed almost immediately that Harry should be given the chance to front his own comedy programme. This was the break that Harry had been waiting for. A 'new to the business' script writer Stan Parkinson set about writing a script and came up with "The Dithering Detective" casting Harry as the owner of a Detective Agency who gets mixed up in a real burglary and finds himself behind bars. After endless alterations to the script, with additional material being written by Ted Taylor, it was finally recorded at Manchester's Dickens Road studios with a supporting cast that included Clive Dunn, William Mervyn, Paddy Edwards & Campbell Singer. It was then sent to London and on Friday 20th March 1959 at 10.45pm Harry's TV career was finally launched. The BBC liked it and commissioned a series of six shows. The problem of who to write the shows was solved by John Ammonds and he gave the job to another unknown (at the time) team of writers Vince Powell & Harry Driver. By the time the second series was commissioned Powell was able to give up his full time job as a stylist in a tailor's shop and concentrate on writing. Powell had been working in Hector Powe's shop in St Ann's Square Manchester and it was him who came up with the idea for the arm & leg window trick which became Harry's trademark. And it was Hector Powe's shop that had just the right kind of window to become the place where the opening sequence for Harry's show was filmed. The shop is now a coffee shop and the window has been

With John Ammonds (left)

Enjoying a drink with agent Billy Marsh

changed to a flush one thereby making it impossible to emulate Harry's trademark. There are, however, other shops in the area that still have the original windows so, if you find yourself in St Anne's Square, why not seek one out and have a go – I did and luckily, those who saw me do it, remembered with affection the times that Harry entered the hearts of the nation by raising his leg and arm at the start of his TV shows.

John Ammonds recalls: -

"Harry said we dared not be successful with the Dithering Detective as it had taken us 2 months to put together and if the bosses liked it we could not sustain it. It was decided that the Detective plot could not be sustained over as full series so Ronnie Taylor came up with the idea of Harry, a housekeeper & an Auntie. When Eric Maswich, who was head of entertainment at the BBC in London, saw the show he was not sure about it as he was expecting a series based around Harry as a detective. He eventually agreed to go ahead with it and granted a series. In the meantime Ronnie Taylor had been given the job of Head of Light Entertainment at Thames TV so could not write the new series. He suggested a writer called Eddie Waring who had written the Huggets but neither Harry nor I liked the script he came up with. Vince Powell had sent me a script for Morecambe & Wise who I was producing at the time but although he had some good ideas I had to write back to say we could not fit him in as we had a full compliment of writers for the Morecambe & Wise shows. Soon after I went to be measured for a suit at Hector Powes tailor shop in Manchester where Vince Powell worked and this chance meeting, when he measured me for the suit, reminded me of his scriptwriting capabilities. When we were having trouble with the script I approached Vince and his partner Harry Driver. At the time they were writing the first scripts for Coronation Street but they said they would take on the project of writing the scripts for the new series. The shows were recorded at the Dickens Road Studios, which were a converted chapel. The area to work in was so small that when the cameras were in position there was no room to move back so most of the shots were done in one position. The small size meant we could only get an audience of 70 people in at any one time so we recorded the sound of 70 people then overdubbed it to make it sound like 140. I always consider that producing Harry was my biggest personal success.

Hamlet? – Surely not !!!

Harry meets Harry.
With good friend Harry Secombe before the signing

One of my favourite memories of Harry was that which took place on the night that President Kennedy was assassinated. We were recording a show at Dickens Rd studios in Manchester, which was to be relayed to London and recorded in London before it was transmitted nationally. The transmission was from London at 7.30 that evening. We had all heard the terrible news about Kennedy and when the decision had to be made as to if the show should be transmitted or not, all the heads of department were at a function so the final decision was made by a junior who gave it the go ahead. When Harry & I were watching the transmission going out he was amazed that it had actually been screened. Emergency Ward 10 had been cut after the first 10 minutes but we were still being shown. During the transmission Harry was getting calls from the newspapers asking if he agreed with the show being aired. As he had to explain, it was not his decision – that being made in London. After the show I had a call from Paul Fox, Head of Current Affairs in London saying that a police escort car was bringing the Leader of the Opposition, Harold Wilson, to the studio for a live link up with the Prime Minister, Alec Douglas Hume in a tribute programme to go out at 10.30. As all the staff had gone home there was only Harry & I left to ensure things went to plan. When Wilson turned up he was wearing an identical Gannex coat to that which Harry had. I introduced him to Harry and he then asked if there was a phone he could use, as he wanted to call the Prime Minister before the start of the programme. The only place was in a small storeroom down the corridor, which was a storeroom for the canteen. So there was the Leader of the Opposition in a small store cupboard, surrounded by tins of corned beef, beans, cauliflower's etc talking to the Prime Minister about the Kennedy assassination – a time when you wish you had a camera. Harry was about to go but then asked if he could come up to the gallery to watch the recording. So with his coat over his shoulder watched the proceedings. After the recording we made our way down from the gallery, Harry carrying his coat, just as Harold Wilson was coming out of the studio. 'Oh thank you Mr Worth for bringing my coat' he said trying to take it off Harry. Harry held on tighter to his coat saying ' No this is my coat ' and for the next few moments a typical Harry Worth routine developed as they debated who's coat it really was."

The real 'Auntie'. Aunt Emma.

One of Harry's favourite pastimes.

Prior to this in 1959 Harry had been in radio in a sequel to In All Directions, a popular earlier series which had starred Peter Ustinov & Peter Jones. In the follow up, *We're in Business*; Harry co-starred as a man with a private income and a shady business partner. Operating from premises of Syd's Café, Peter Jones schemed to use Harry's money to finance his own, doomed to failure, get rich quick schemes. Also in the series were Irene Handle and Dick Emery. In 1976 he starred in the radio series Things Could Be Worse and Thirty Minutes Worth first heard in 1963 was revived over 20 years later, introducing him to a whole new generation of listeners.

The Trouble With Harry in 1960, in which Harry was a struggling author, was his first national TV show, his first being shown in the north only. All of Harry's shows until 1965 were produced in Manchester. In the show Harry was cast as a timid, ineffectual aspiring author whose aunt keeps him on the straight and narrow. Aunt was played by Noel Hood and the housekeeper Doris by Paddy Edwards. The series was written by Frank Roscoe & Ronnie Taylor and was produced by John Ammonds and ran for 6 episodes.

Here's Harry followed towards the end of 1960 which had Harry living at 52 Acacia Avenue, Woodbridge. This was probably Harry's most successful series running for 60 episodes from Oct 1960 to Dec 1965. Harry later became the first comedian to feature in a series over 100 times and in 1962 was awarded the Variety Club of Great Britain BBC TV Personality of the Year. *Here's Harry* had a cast of regular faces including Patrick Newell, Vi Stevens, Stuart Saunders, Deryck Guyler, Ivor Salter, Jack Woolgar & Reginald Marsh. It was written by Eddie Maguire, Vince Powell, Harry Driver & Frank Roscoe. John Ammonds produced the first 6 series with John Street producing the final one. Ivor Slaney wrote the music that was to be heard being hummed on many lips for years to follow.

Harry's auntie, Mrs Amelia Prendergast, was by then a regular character in the series but only actually appeared in one episode, that being 'The Portrait' in 1963. Auntie was in fact based on Harry's real life aunt – Emma Arnold. She lived in Shepperton, Australia after moving from England just before Christmas in 1928. Nine of Harry's aunts and uncles emigrated. Two uncles John & Bob Crick worked in the coal mines in Sydney. Harry, Kay & Jobyna went to visit Aunt Emma in 1969 as part of a round-the-world holiday. In June 1970 he flew her to Britain for a holiday and to meet friends &

Judging a beauty contest with Erc Morely, Cilla Black, Sid James & Val Doonican.

Harry's stage act.

relations she had not seen since she emigrated all those years ago. It was a media gift when advantage was taken of Harry meeting Auntie and introducing her to the world. Aunt Emma returned to Australia where she died on 27th August 1970 aged 84.

Harry Worth was the follow up to the long running *Here's Harry*. In this series writer Ronnie Taylor took Harry further afield than in his previous domestic encounters and in the penultimate episode almost married him off. The series was produced by Graeme Muir, Duncan Wood, Eric Fawcett & Douglas Argent. It ran from Oct 1966 to Jan 1970

The Harry Worth show continued at the BBC until, in 1970, the Network Controller decided that the show should end, the excuse being given that it was ' Old Fashioned Comedy '. Thankfully that was not the end of Harry's TV career.

Vince Powell was responsible for Harry's return to television this time with ITV luring Harry away from the BBC. In the series *Thirty Minutes Worth* which was an extension of a previous radio series of the same title. The series was basically the same as the BBC shows seeing Harry bumbling his way through various exploits and frustrating the various supporting casts. There were 3 series over 13 months between 13th Oct 1972 and 28th Nov 1973.

The series was written jointly by Mike Craig, Ron McDonnell and Lawrie Kinsley.

William G Stewart, of 15 to One fame produced the second series, who remembers: -

"Over the past 45 years I have been lucky enough to work with some of the nicest people in the entertainment business, but none nicer than Harry Worth. He was a gentle man, with an air of vulnerability about him. On one occasion he told me that a tough young East End actor playing a policeman who had to question Harry in a police cell, frightened him – and would I ask the actor not to be so hard at every rehearsal. There was a lot of the screen Harry Worth in the real Harry Worth – or should it be the other way round? He attracted affection from everyone who knew him. And, apart from his television series, anyone who never saw his ventriloquist act missed an absolute treat. You couldn't see his lips move, but his voice and that of his dummy were identical. He was a very nice man".

Henry Boot reporting for duty.

In 1972, Michael Mills had recently resigned as BBC's Head of Comedy to concentrate on producing. Mills saw Harry as an ideal choice for his new project – the TV adaptation of Evelyn Waugh's classic novel Scoop about a country bumpkin style correspondent called William Boot. Eyes were raised at the casting of Harry Worth but Mills counted on the fact that Boot's accident-prone character was similar to that of Harry's sitcom character. It was performed like a sitcom in front of an audience who were baffled by the storyline and expected a typical Harry Worth comedy. Despite Barry Took's efforts to produce a TV translation, the casting & style of the series worked against the production and it was not seen as a success. Sheila Hancock, Brian Oulton, Kenneth J Warren, John Junkin, Gerald Flood, Meredith Edwards & Sinead Cusack made up the cast and the series ran for 7 episodes between Oct & Nov 1972. It was also Harry's first full colour series. Prior to this, Paramount pictures had asked Harry if he was interested in playing William Boot in the film version of Scoop. He was taken out to a slap up lunch by the company and, with not much persuading, said yes to the project. They drew up a contract and then set about getting the screenplay written. After the eighth draft of the screenplay they were not satisfied so paid Harry off and that was the closest he came to being a film star, although he did have a small part in one. He appeared in David Leans 1948 production of Oliver Twist and can be seen as a torch carrying extra chasing Bill Sykes over a bridge. He got four nights work at 4 guineas a night (£4.20) and thought it was wonderful.

In 1974 Harry returned to the more domestic type of comedy. He was cast as a brush salesman moving into a boarding house run by a widow, Mrs Maybury. His attempts to do all the right things for all the right reasons were thwarted by his inability to understand the ways of the world. Lally Bowers played Mrs Maybury & Reginald Marsh her brother George. The series was written by Ronnie Taylor, George Layton, Jonathan Lynn, Spike Mullins & Peter Robinson. William G Stewart produced and directed. It ran for 8 episodes from 22 April 1974 to 17th June 1974.

After being away from TV screens on a regular basis for five years, Harry rejected a number of scripts for his 'comeback' before finally settling on How's Your Father? He was cast as recently widowed, middle aged Harry Matthews left with the problems of

With Debbie Cumming & Giles Watling in How's Your Father.

raising two teenage children, Shirley, 16 and Martin, 19. Those problems, of course, seeming more dramatic and confusing to Harry than to anyone else. Debbie Cumming played Shirley & Giles Watling, Martin. Also appearing was Fanny Carby & Sonia Graham. The writers were Pam Valentine & Michael Ashton. Graeme Muir produced and directed. It ran for 2 series over 13 episodes between 27th Feb 1979 & 3rd April 1979 & 18th July 1980 & 29th August 1980.

Debbie Cumming remembers Harry with affection: -

"We always used to do our script read through on a Sunday afternoon at a boys club in Chiswick. I started by taking a cake along which soon became the norm as Harry looked forward to seeing which sort I was going to arrive with. I remember Harry always wore a cardigan at rehearsals but always wore it off the shoulder so it hung right down almost to his knees. He was a great joker on set and during one scene I had had an argument with my brother and had to storm out of the room. As I went trough the door there was Harry sitting on an imaginary staircase. I just collapsed into fits of laughter and we had to do several retakes before I had composed myself. Harry loved to visit Harry Ramsdens when we were filming in Leeds. One day he said he would love to see what the youngsters got up to at night so we arranged to take him to a night-club. As soon as we girls formed the normal circle on the floor with our handbags Harry was up there dancing in the middle, surprising us all and becoming the clubs star attraction of the night. I remember visiting his home where he still had his miner's helmet and lamp on display in his study and I recall his large collection of J.B. Priestly books. Working with Harry was a lesson in timing, expecting the unexpected and, of course, Happy Days"

Harry's last TV series saw his return to the BBC in 1980 in *Oh Happy Band!* Where he starred as the leader of a brass band in the small town of Nettlebridge. He and his band are seen attempting various schemes to thwart the building of a nearby airport while managing to indulge in a spot of brass-band music (actually provided by the Aldershot Brass Ensemble). There was a large cast that included Jonathan Cecil, John Horsley, Billy Burden, Tom Mennard & Harold Bennett.

The cast of 'Oh Happy Band' including Jonathan Cecil, Tom Mennard, Billy Burdon & John Horsley with the Aldershot Brass Ensemble.

The writers were David Croft & Jeremy Lloyd and David Croft produced the series. It ran for 8 episodes between 3rd Sept & 8th Oct 1980.

Harry & Kay had moved from Brighton 1955 to Woodmansterne in Surrey and a couple of years later to Kenley – also in Surrey. In 1963 they moved to Berkhamsted where they were to remain and the house was duly named 'Arisden' (Harry's Den). They chose the area because they remembered it from their time at Halton and it was also the nearest town and the place where they went to the cinema and tearoom.

Jo recalls: -

"Dad didn't care much for staying in hotels so when the summer holidays came around he would rent a house near where his summer season was and we would pack the house along with the dog, rabbit, goldfish all into the back of mums Ford Anglia. How we ever did it I am not sure but we got there. Mum and Dad had a lovely memory of those days for me. We were on tour with the Laurel & Hardy show and Mum & Dad had been invited to a function. Stan & Ollie had also been invited but were not keen to go. The problem with a babysitter was soon overcome as Mum & Dad went off to the event leaving me with my new-found babysitters Laurel & Hardy. Onscreen, the biggest accident-prone pair around – offscreen, the kindest gentlest pair you could meet."

Harry enjoyed a constant demand for theatre and pantomime work, Panto being where he had first met Kay, and had the honour of appearing in three Royal Variety Performances in 1958, 1960 & 1980. He often appeared in Panto with his good friend Peter Butterworth (of Carry On fame). During his time on stage he encouraged and helped many a newcomer to the business. Comedian Jimmy Cricket remembers: -

"I worked with Harry in "Jack & The Beanstalk" at the Hippodrome, Birmingham in 1984. Having long been an admirer of Harry's since my teenage years, it was a dream fulfilled to be actually working with the maestro himself. He didn't disappoint. I probably laughed more during that pantomime than any other. We got a deal at a local hotel, so from breakfast time to midnight we were like giggling schoolboys. It was my first big Panto (Cilla Black was topping the bill) and to have someone of Harry's ilk in my corner was a g

Harry with Peter Butterworth in Old King Cole

And with Jimmy Cricket, Cilla Black, Paul Squires & Gareth Hunt.

godsend. I was also just breaking into TV and Harry's advice dispensed into the wee small hours of the morning was invaluable. As he reminded me he was fortunate to have had over ten years where his TV show was at the top and he was doing sell out business in theatres during summer seasons and pantomime. We were big fans of Billy Dainty and Harry told me how he was the first to get Billy to play dame in Panto. Billy then went on to become one of the best dames in the country. Harry also enthralled us with stories of Laurel & Hardy, how they were gentle, beautiful people. Stan would actually stand in the wings and make creative suggestions to Harry.

Harry's warm, gentle character and clean honest to goodness humour brought him legions of fans of all ages. He was loved by people both inside & outside the business and his place in show business history is assured."

In 1963 one of the biggest accolades was bestowed upon Harry when he was chosen, as the subject for *This Is Your Life,* then presented by Eamon Andrews. Stan Laurel had been asked to appear as a guest on the show and although he wanted to had to decline due to ill health. He died 2 years later on 23rd February 1965. During his last moments he had beckoned the nurse tending him and said as he lay in bed ' I'd rather be skiing than doing this'. 'Do you ski Mr Laurel?' asked the nurse. 'No' replied Stan. 'But I'd rather be skiing than doing this' A few minutes later he was dead.

In 1970 Harry was asked to play, on stage, Elmer P. Dowd, the character portrayed by James Stewart in the film version of Harvey, where he is constantly visited by an imaginary six foot white rabbit. Michael Grade remembers: -

"The production company had the touring rights but still had to obtain the authors permission but a letter sent saw the permission refused. They rang Mary Chase, the author, in Colorado and she explained the reason she had not granted the rights was that she had had a dream that it would not succeed. After gentle persuasion however, the right was granted and Harry went on to appear in its successful run.

Harry was always conservative in what he did, he could not be categorised – he was totally unique. Eric Morecambe's favourite line was when Harry was doing his vent act and he used to say 'I do assure you that it is me speaking and to prove this I do allow my lips to move'.

This Is Your Life 28ᵗʰ October 1963. Eamon Andrews sprung the surprise on
Harry assisted by Kay, Jobyna and hiding behind the flowers- Suzy.

On stage with Billy Dainty

Should I have done that?
Playing for charity

Billy Marsh labelled Harry as having the 'Going Home on the Train syndrome'. Harry used to travel to Billy Marsh's office by train to discuss the next years work They would talk, over lunch, about what he wanted to do in the coming year, the summer season options, the TV work etc and by the end of lunch it was all done a dusted. Harry would then leave for the train journey home. Once he was back home he would ring Billy and say 'Thanks for the lunch but I have thought about what we discussed and I'm not sure I want to do this or that' and so the whole thing was unravelled and it was back to the drawing board after he had thought about it on the train. He was a lovely, lovely man."

Harry admitted to having one thing in common with his screen character and that was not being able to remember people's names. *"If I see someone on TV fairly often the face registers with me, but I usually forget where I have seen them and assume that I know them personally. It is terrible when I go to the BBC. I walk down the corridor saying Hello – Nice to see you again to the weatherman, the political correspondent, even the lades who do Play School. I did it to Esther Rantzen one day. I said Hello love - nice to see you again after all this time! How are you getting on? Oh, very well she said looking totally blank. Then it dawned on me that she hadn't a clue who I was and I had never met her before in my life."*

Harry had no illusions about the glamour and glitter of showbusiness "We *sing 'There's No Business Like Show Business' but that's a lot of rubbish. Every business is like show business. They all have their ups and downs. The only thing that makes what we do special is that we can go on playing Cowboys and Indians all our lives. And I can think of no happier and more enjoyable way of spending your life.* One of Harry's regrets was turning down a part that had been written for him in the film 'Those Magnificent Men In Their Flying Machines' which was later played by Tony Hancock. He recalled *"I regret not doing it. I suppose I may have been too cautious, but at the time, I thought it was only going to be a small cameo role".*

When Harry wasn't working he spent his time with his family on their 24ft cabin cruiser 'Seaker' moored on the River Thames which he owned from 1973-75 later buying

Ahoy there!!

'Ozymandias in 1975. His favourite sports to watch were football and cricket and he would often go and sit in his car to listen to the commentaries as in the house he could not concentrate as Kay would always be talking to him. He always listened to the radio more than he watched TV. His love of cricket saw him playing for the Lord Taverners. He was a keen golfer and he and his Grandson Dane belonged to Berkhamsted Golf Club. He often played a round with friends such as Jimmy Tarbuck, Edmund Hockridge, Harry Secombe and many more. He loved the cinema and would take Jo whenever he could as she shared his love of films. Kay did not go very often because she would always fall asleep during the film. Harry loved watching plays and was a great Alan Ayckbourn fan and his favourite singers were Frank Sinatra and Shirley Bassey. He would also take the family on a holiday abroad each year and, when he was working on the cruise liners, the family would go as well. Whenever something new came out Harry was the first to want it but only ever wanted it on loan. When the staff in Curry's saw him coming they would hide. He would have a TV for a few weeks then say 'I'm not sure about it – Can I try another one? He also hated being recognised so when walking around Berkhamsted he would hold a handkerchief over his face pretending to have a cold. Eventually the locals would get used to it and know it was him anyway saying 'Here comes Harry again with another cold!'

Although the 60's were his golden years, when his TV show was at its peak, Harry's stage act was always in demand. He lived to work. When he was doing the television shows he would be at the studios all day and then come home and often work on the scripts until five o'clock in the morning.

In 1983 Harry was diagnosed with cancer of the spine found during a routine operation, but didn't want to give into it and carried on working. After treatment he was convinced he was cured but it was on stage at Bromley in Kent, appearing with Kathy Staff (Nora Batty in Last of the Summer Wine) that his final illness caught up with him. He arrived home one night and said his legs didn't feel as though they belonged to him. He insisted going to work the next day because they had no understudy. When he arrived home he virtually fell in the house. It took Kay an hour to get him upstairs. He was rushed to hospital and had major surgery to remove a tumour from his spine, spending 10 weeks in hospital. He never wanted

Possibly the last photo of Harry taken with Norman Lovett at a charity event a few weeks before he passed away.

(Photo courtesy of Norman Lovatt)

people to visit him in hospital but eventually Kathy Staff just turned up and he was delighted to see her.

Kay converted the dining room of their home into a bedroom and Harry went home in a wheelchair and, despite doctors warnings that he might never walk again, was determined to get back on his feet. He did all his exercises and within six months was able to walk with a zimmer frame. Then, one day, he shouted to Kay "Quick, I can walk!' He could walk 2 steps and with the help of crutches and stick he got going again.

He was asked to do a television commercial, which involved kicking a bucket over, and he was determined to do it. On day of filming the studio sent a car for him and as he climbed in he shouted to Kay 'Catch this' and threw her his stick. He was determined nobody should see him use it.

He eventually did a concert in Cambridge and was delighted to be working again. 'I'm working again so everything is fine' was his attitude. But the tumour reappeared and this time when Harry was rushed to hospital the doctor told Kay there was nothing more they could do for him. The surgeon told Harry that he was going to be a very sick man and would never walk again. Harry asked Kay to go out of the room for a few minutes – he wanted to be on his own. When she went back he was his usual cheerful self and never complained once. Kay was determined to take Harry home to die – despite the doctors' advice that he should stay in hospital. So with the help of the Ian Rennie Nurses in Berkhamsted he came home. Although he knew he was dying he remained cheerful and became very interested in the birds, rabbits & badgers in the garden. He was on 26 tablets a day including morphine and heroin at the end. He called Kay 'Mrs Thatcher' because she had to be a bit bossy, making sure he took his tablets. Kay believed he struggled to stay alive for her 70th birthday. He had asked Jo to order flowers for Kay and asked for a bottle of champagne to be opened when the two morning nurses came in and we all had a glass. When the other nurses came in the evening, we opened another bottle – it was a lovely special day. It was the last time that Harry got out of bed. He lived for another week but was only partially conscious. Jo & Kay stayed with him all the time just sleeping in the chairs next to him, holding his hands. On 20th July 1989 Harry passed away in the company of the people he loved. He told Jo, in

Harry & Kay

the days before he lost consciousness *"I've done everything I've wanted to do, I've had a wonderful life and your mum has helped me all the way."*

That is why Kay asked for Wonderful World to be played at his cremation service and his memorial service. It was one of the tunes he used in his act, and it summed up his attitude to life. Kay later recalled: -

"I knew just how hard Harry had battled against the disease for the last 6 years of his life, and how, when the end came, it was a release from pain and suffering. It was only in the last few days, when he was semi-conscious, that he stopped singing and joking. He never once complained, and he must have been in terrible pain. We were together for over 42 years, and it was a very, very happy marriage. I don't think people realise how many good marriages there are in showbusiness – you only hear about the bad ones. When I look back, I'm so grateful for all those years together and the happiness we had. At home Harry and I were a double act. He was always careful with money - we lived very comfortably but never above our means. In the sixties, when he was at the peak of his fame he was paying 97.5p in the £1 income tax, so it was impossible to be rich. He took care of everything – it is because he did that I am able to stay in this house now."

The cremation was held at Amersham to a packed congregation. The BBC agreed to transport the Grimethorpe Colliery Band to London for his memorial service held at All Souls Church, Langham Place, London on 6th Oct 1989, which set the northern tone for the packed congregation. They played an arrangement of "Ilkley Moor Baht'at'" and the Ivor Slaney composition of Harry's signature tune "Here Harry".

Sir Harry Secombe closed the service and the final words of this book are left to his quote

"Harry has left behind a legacy of laughter and millions of people have all been enriched by his presence here on earth"

**On set during the filming of The Overdraft from
Here's Harry 1961**

Appendix 1

The TV Shows

Here's Harry

Cast
Harry Worth - Harry Worth

Crew
Eddie Maguire - Writer
Vince Powell – Writer
Harry Driver - Writer
Frank Roscoe - Writer (series 1-6); Ronnie Taylor (series 7); Lew Schwarz (short special)
John Ammonds - Producer (series 1-6)
John Street - Producer (series 7)
Dennis Main Wilson - Producer (short special)

Transmission Details
Number of episodes: 60 Length: 59 x 30 mins · 1 x short special
Series One (6) 11 Oct-15 Nov 1960, Tue 7.30pm
Short special part of Christmas Night With The Stars 25 Dec 1960, Sun 6pm
Series Two (5) 4 May-8 June 1961, Thu 7.30pm
Series Three (8) 14 Nov 1961-2 Jan 1962, Tue mostly 8pm
Series Four (12) 8 Oct-24 Dec 1962, Mon mostly 8pm
Series Five (10) 25 Oct-27 Dec 1963, Fri 7.45pm
Series Six (8) 13 Oct-1 Dec 1964, BBC1 Tue 8pm
Series Seven (10) 8 Oct-10 Dec 1965, BBC1 Fri 7.30pm

The Trouble With Harry

Cast
Harry Worth - Harry Worth
Noel Hood - Aunt Victoria
Paddy Edwards – Doris

Crew
Ronnie Taylor - Writer (5)
Ronnie Taylor - Writer (1)
Frank Roscoe - Writer (1)
John Ammonds - Producer

Transmission Details
Number of episodes: 6 Length: 30 mins
1 Jan-4 Feb 1960, Fri 7.30pm then Thu 6.20pm

Harry and Mrs Mills

Harry Worth

Cast
Harry Worth - Harry Worth

Crew
Ronnie Taylor - Writer
Graeme Muir - Producer (series 1 & 2)
Duncan Wood - Producer (series 2 & 3)
Eric Fawcett - Producer (series 2)
Douglas Argent - Producer (series 4)

Transmission Details
Number of episodes: 38 Length: 37 x 30 mins · 1 x short special
Series One (10) 28 Oct-30 Dec 1966 · BBC1 Fri 7.30pm
Series Two (9) 3 Oct-28 Nov 1967 · BBC1 Tue 7.30pm
Short special · part of Christmas Night With The Stars 25 Dec 1967 · BBC1 Mon 6.40pm
Series Three (10) 21 Oct-23 Dec 1968 · BBC1 Mon 7.30pm
Series Four (8) 18 Nov 1969-13 Jan 1970 · BBC1 Tue 7.30pm

Scoop

Cast

Harry Worth - William Boot
Sheila Hancock - Mrs Stitch
Brian Oulton - Salter
Kenneth J Warren - Lord Copper
John Junkin - Baldwin
Gerald Flood - John Boot
Gerald Flood - John Boot
Meredith Edwards - Uncle Theodore
Sinead Cusack – Katchen

Crew

Evelyn Waugh - Creator
Barry Took - Adapter / Writer
Michael Mills – Producer

Transmission Details
Number of episodes: 7 Length: 30 mins
8 Oct-19 Nov 1972 · BBC2 Sun 9pm

Harry on the way to a store opening

Thirty Minutes Worth

Cast
Harry Worth - Harry Worth

Crew
Vince Powell - Script Editor
Mike Craig
Lawrie Kinsley
Ron McDonnell
Frank Roscoe
Roy Tuvey
Maurice Sellar
George Martin
Johnnie Mortimer
Brian Cooke
Jim Wilde
Dave Freeman
Ronnie Taylor
Les Chatfield - Director / Producer (series 1 & 3)
William G Stewart - Director / Producer (series 2)

Transmission Details
Number of episodes: 23 Length: 22 x 30 mins · 1 x short special
Series One (8) 31 Oct-19 Dec 1972, Tue around 7pm
Special (colour) part of All-Star Comedy Carnival 25 Dec 1972, Mon 5.45pm
Series Two (6) 4 July-8 Aug 1973, Wed 8pm
Series Three (8) 3 Oct-28 Nov 1973, Wed 8pm

My Name Is Harry Worth

Cast
Harry Worth - Harry Worth
Lally Bowers - Mrs Maybury
Reginald Marsh - George Bailey

Crew
Ronnie Taylor - Writer (4)
George Layton - Writer (3)
Jonathan Lynn - Writer (3)
Spike Mullins - Writer (1)
Peter Robinson - Writer (1)
William G Stewart - Director / Producer

Transmission Details
Number of episodes: 8 Length: 30 mins
22 Apr-17 June 1974, Mon 8pm

ALHAMBRA
BRADFORD 1953

Secretary: ROWLAND HILL   Managing Director: FRANCIS LAIDLER   Phone: 27097   Man.: GEORGE BAINES

6.0   Week of MONDAY, MAY 25th   **8.15**

FIRST TIME HERE OF THE NEW STAR
COMEDIAN FROM "VARIETY FANFARE"!

KEN PLATT

I'M NOT STOPPING!

AND BIG ALL LAUGHTER BILL!

MORECAMBE AND WISE
FOOLS RUSH IN
DIRECT FROM THE LONDON PALLADIUM

THE 4 D'S
Music Maestro Please

LESLIE FLACK AND ALLAN LUCAS
BRITAIN'S GREATEST HIGH-SPEED DANCERS

PENNY "SERENADE" NICHOLLS AND BILLY MERRIN

HARRY WORTH
A FIGURE OF SPEECH

THE KERBSIDERS
BROTHER CAN YOU SPARE A DIME

THE CASSANDRAS

Harry

Cast
Harry Worth
Josephine Tewson

Crew
Ronnie Taylor - Writer
James Moir - Producer

Transmission Details
Number of episodes: 1 Length: 40 mins
12 Nov 1976, BBC2 Fri 9.30pm

How's Your Father

Cast
Harry Worth - Harry Matthews
Debby Cumming - Shirley Matthews
Giles Watling - Martin Matthews
Fanny Carby - Vera Blacker (series 1)
Sonia Graham - Mrs Simkins (series 2)

Crew
Pam Valentine - Writer
Michael Ashton - Writer
Graeme Muir - Director (9)
Don Clayton - Director (4)
Graeme Muir – Producer

Transmission Details
Number of episodes: 13 Length: 30 mins
Series One (6) 27 Feb-3 Apr 1979, Tue mostly 8.30pm
Series Two (7) 18 July-29 Aug 1980, Fri 7.30pm

Blackpool fun

Oh Happy Band

Cast

Harry Worth - Harry Worth
Jonathan Cecil - Mr Herbert
John Horsley - Mr Braithwaite
Billy Burden - Mr Sowerby
Tom Mennard - Mr Pilgrim
Tony Sympson - Mr Giles
Jan Holden - Mrs Draper
Harold Bennett – Vicar
Moira Foot - Glenda
PeggyAnn Clifford - Mrs Tickford
Margaret Clifton - Miss Mayhew
Myrtle Devenish – Winnie
Jeffrey Segal - Man from the Ministry
Ronnie Brody - Mr Turtle
Mollie Maureen - Vicar's wife

Crew
Jeremy Lloyd - Writer
David Croft - Writer
David Croft – Producer

Transmission Details
Number of episodes: 6 Length: 30 mins
3 Sep-8 Oct 1980, BBC1 Wed 8.30pm

A relaxing moment with Kay

Appendix 2

Harry's Vent Act 1950

F- Fotheringhay   C- Clarence   H- Harry

H Excuse me.

F Oh, go away I'm fast asleep.

H I'm sorry, I have to disturb you.

F Exactly who are you?

H I'm the waiter.

F Exactly what are you waiting for?

H I`m waiting for you to pay the bill.

F I say, that's rather unfortunate.

H You mean you haven't enough?

F You're exaggerating – I haven't anything.

H You should have money.

F I couldn't agree more – I had a little until yesterday.

H You should learn to make a little go a long way.

F Yes, Is your name Stracey?

H No, you say you had money?

F Yes, and then I had a date.

H With a girl?

F Yes, what a smasher!

H Tell me, where did you get hold of her?

F Oh, anywhere, she wasn't particular.

H I mean, where did you meet her?

F Well, I was walking along Picallily

H You mean Piccadily.

F I said Picallily.

H Picallily is mustard.

F Yes, so is Piccadilly – didn't you know?

H Was she a good girl?

F I can't afford the other kind.

H I mean was she pretty?

F She had everyhing Larna Turner has.

H Good.

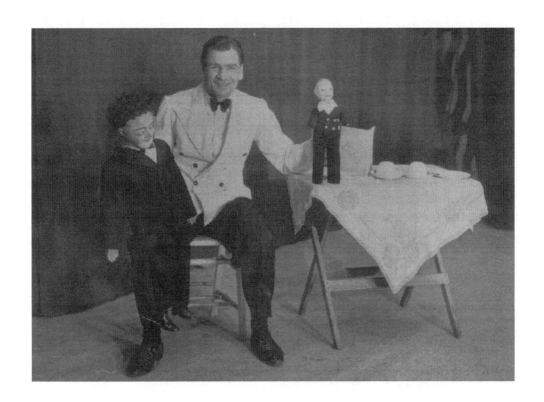

An early shot with Clarence & Fotheringhay.

**Poster from Harry's collection where he has written
"1st professional engagement £8. Including Harry Worth."**

F	Unfortunately, she had it thirty years longer. She was nothing really but a little Gold Digger – do you know what I spent on that girl?
H	I've no idea.
F	One and three-pence ha'penny.
H	One and three-pence ha'penny isn't much to spend on a girl.
F	That's all she had.
H	That's all she had – don't you work?
F	What?
H	I said do you work?
F	Aren't you being rather unpleasant?
H	I don't think so, a lot of people work.
F	Yes, I know, it takes all sorts to make a world. I do work on extremely rare occasions – coronation days etc.
H	How about your Father?
F	He used to work in a factory
H	Why did he leave?
F	The manager said something he didn't like.
H	What was that?
F	Get out and stay out.
H	What is he doing now?
F	He opened a jewelers shop.
H	Good, How's he doing?
F	Six months - the shop wasn't his.
H	Crime don't pay.
F	The hours are good.
H	Why don't you sell you suit?
F	This is my demob suit.
H	Were you in the Army?
F	No.
H	The navy?
F	No.
H	What were you in?
F	Actually, The Royal Air Force.
H	A very fine service.
F	Wizard.
H	I was in the Air Force during the war.#
F	Were you really?

One of Harry's favourite pantomime roles.

H	Yes.
F	Really?
H	Yes.
F	How jolly – no wonder we nearly lost.
H	It's obvious you were bred for the Navy.
F	Oh, I don't know, my Grandfather was a very fine sailor – you've heard of the Dead Sea?
H	Yes, Everybody's heard of the Dead Sea
F	My Grandfather shot it.
H	A remarkable character your Grandfather.
F	Rather, he knew the exact moment he was going to die.
H	Did he?
F	Yes, the judge told him.
H	Did he ever go on a cruise?
F	Every night he went on the booze.
H	Oh, he drank.
F	Yes.
H	Why did he drink.
F	He didn't really know what else to do with it.
H	I've no sympathy for a man that gets drunk every night.
F	A man that gets drunk every night doesn't really need your sympathy.
H	No – I say, who is this hiding behind the menu?
F	Oh yes. I should introduce you – that is Clarence.
H	Clarence?
F	Yes, he carried the torch at the Olympic games.
H	He's not very old.
F	No, there's an obvious reason – he hasn't lived very long. He's five years of age – he's in standard one.
H	Really.
F	Yes, when I was in standard one I was different to the other five year olds.
H	Were you?
F	Yes , I was ten.
H	Clarence, your brother Freddie has no – are you listening Clarence?
C	Yes.
H	Are you sure?
C	Yes.
H	Are you well?

Panto rehearsals

A quick tune

C	Yes
F	He's rather inclined to be a "Yes Man"
H	Your brother Freddie has no money, woud you care to lend him any?
C	No.
H	No?
C	No
F	Did he say no?
C	Yes.
F	Thank you Mr Molotov
H	Would you do a little work to earn some money?
C	Work
H	Work
C	Work
H	Yes
C	No
F	Jolly good – he's got the right idea.

At this point Harry would close his vent act going through the routine of putting the dummies away.

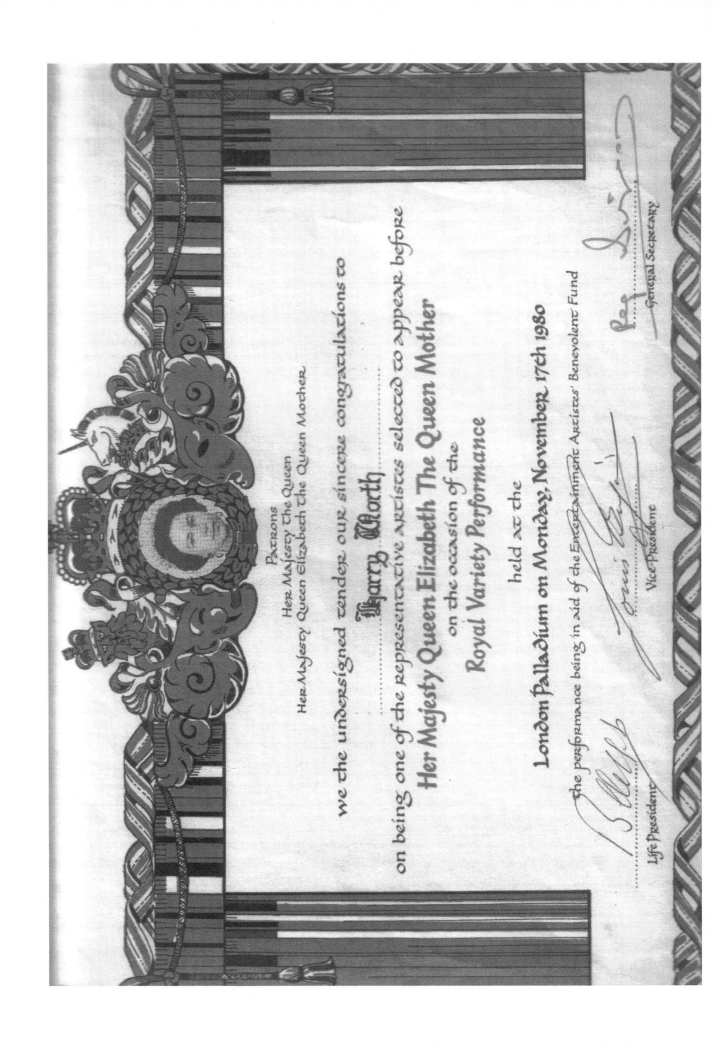

Patrons

Her Majesty The Queen
Her Majesty Queen Elizabeth The Queen Mother

we the undersigned tender our sincere congratulations to

Harry Worth

on being one of the representative artistes selected to appear before

Her Majesty Queen Elizabeth The Queen Mother

on the occasion of the

Royal Variety Performance

held at the

London Palladium on Monday, November 17th 1980

the performance being in aid of the Entertainment Artistes' Benevolent Fund

Life President

Vice-President

General Secretary

Appendix 2

Cabaret Act

Play on music   **Harry Enters:-**

Good evening. Very nice to see you and err ....

Oh – There you are (Glasses). I'll confess to you here and now – I don't need these – only for seeing. And I think it's important to mention this – whether it's on stage, radio, screen or cabaret – sometime or another – there must be a dull moment. Well here I am. And may I say it's nice to be with you here in ....

Now are you sitting comfortably? Are you in the right seats? I tell you why I ask. I went to the cinema the other night. I went in in the dark and sat on a man's hat. He was very annoyed – his head was still in it. Oh he was angry. For a moment I thought he was going to hit me. But he had his lovely wife with him – and she hit me! Oh – I'm sorry. I owe you an apology. Apart from being here I haven't introduced myself. And you might mistake me for one of the others – and they wouldn't like it. And furthermore – I haven't thanked you for that wonderful welcome you have just given me. I do appreciate it. And I should – I know what's coming!

Now my name is..... (looking for note)....... Harry Worth! And I am a comedian.

 I tell you that I'm a comedian now, not only to save arguments later on, but you never know – some lady in the audience might turn to her husband and ask ...."What is he?" And he, poor man, might forget himself – and tell her! And for

BERNARD DELFONT
presents
(for Prime Presentations Limited)

SHOW TIME

HARRY WORTH

at the NORTH PIER PAVILION BLACKPOOL

Programme One Shilling

that – the poor man could lose his wife – and it's hard to lose a wife... hard??? It's impossible.

I beg your pardon ladies – it was only a joke. Not a very good one but nevertheless – a joke. Incidentally, if you don't like jokes I tell you tonight – don't blame the people who wrote them – they've been dead thirty years.

But I shouldn't make fun of wives. I didn't know what real happiness was until I got married – and then it was too late. No – my wife's a good woman – honest woman – respectable woman – it's very monotonous. But you may say to yourself – lots of people talk to themselves .... I talk to myself. It's boring. You see one day I might say something important and if I do I'd love to be there.

You may be saying to yourself - Harry Worth – I've never heard of him. And do let me assure you – I am not making a comeback. I haven't been anywhere. Because I'm assuming you've seen me on television – not everybody watches television. They go out and enjoy themselves. And you can't blame them with these old films they keep showing. I saw the midnight movie the other night – it was so old it was a shame to keep it up so late. Did you see it? It was called "Henry the Eighth". Do you know who was playing Henry the Eighth? – Henry the Ninth.

Now at this point it was suggested I sing you a song. Which is a great pity, because you have done nothing wrong to me. Don't misunderstand me I did sing a song once – a very sympathetic song... and the way I sang it – it was pitiful. I was appearing at a little theatre in Barnsley. Please – don't think for one moment I'm going to make fun of Barnsley. You never know – there may be someone here from there- and if there is – it's not your fault. I don't mind telling you here and now – I was born in Barnsley. But funny things happen in London. Not a bad place – theatres, shops, cinemas and if it's night life you are after – you're only two hundred miles from London.

However – I walked onto this stage in Barnsley- and the theatre was packed – right up to the third row. Lovely audience- sitting –more or less as you are now – and I had a feeling that they didn't like me. Not by the hatred on their faces – it was the way they were sharpening knives on the backs of the chairs. I thought 'Oh – I'd better tell

a joke before I sing – and make them laugh '. And so I told a joke. And a man did laugh.....
they turned him out and said he was drunk. I didn't mind him going out. I never mind when
audiences walk out on me. It's when they start walking towards me. I must tell you – the man
went out – but his wife stayed. Poor woman – she couldn't find her shoes anywhere. However
– there's always a silver lining. I started singing and it was wonderful. All the hatred left there
faces and was replaced with Agony! Oh they were suffering. I couldn't bear to watch them. I
went off. And they didn't ask me to come back for any applause. Ask me? They sat there and
dared me to! It frightened me. I ran to my dressing room. Dressing room. A nail on the wall.
And the manager of the theatre was waiting for me. He was a nice man. He liked me. He
watched me twice. He didn't believe it the first time. I can see him now. Standing as you
might say – there! Very smart man. Evening dress, white tie, tails – brown boots – flat cap! I
thought I'd better make some excuse for not doing well on stage – I'll pretend I'm ill. So I said
to him – "Oh I do feel funny". He said , "Then get back on before it wears off". Very nice man.

BELL NOTE FROM PIANO: INTO PARODY: EVERYTHING HAPPENS TO ME

AFTER PARODY

And now...... (PIANIST PLAYS ARPEGGIO) (HARRY LOOKS ACROSS)

Oh yes.... Do come forward......Ladies & Gentlemen. I'd like you to meet .... my

pianist. I think I should tell you he has played for the singing of .. (TO PIANIST)

..pardon? Yes – I know – I did promise you can do a piano solo, and when the

moment is right you can do it.

I should mention that Mr .... has played for Frankie Vaughan, Tom Jones, Harry

Secombe – and you've enjoyed it, haven't you? (PIANIST NODS) Now are you ready to

play for me?

(PIANIST PRODUCES TWO STRANDS OF COTTON WOOL WHICH HE STUFFS INTO HIS

EARS AND RETREATS.

You can't blame him – he loves good music.

And now I think I ought to tell you a joke, and before anyone says "About time too" -

I'll press on.

On board Canberra with Ted Moult, Pete Murray,

Leslie Thomas & Norman Vaughan.

With Prince Charles at a Royal Variety Show.

This is a joke about a man who goes to see a psychiatrist.... Oh by the way – as I've heard this joke before, when I get to the end of it I probably won't laugh. I thought I'd mention that – I wouldn't like you to think I'd missed the point.

Anyway, this man walked into a psychiatrists consulting room and the psychiatrist said , "Good morning – what can I do for you?" And the man said, "I'd like to ask you two questions." And the psychiatrist said " Yes of course – what is the first one?". And the man said, "Is it possible for a man to fall in love with an elephant?" And the psychiatrist said "Of course not. What is the second question?" And the man said...........

ORCHESTRA: QUICK CHORUS: WITH OR WITHOUT PIANIST. APPLAUSE

And this man said, "Do you know anybody who wants to buy a large engagement ring?"

You can't help laughing can you? Although I must say you are making a very good effort.

My father warned me about the stage. Oh course – I haven't mentioned my father to you have I. No you haven't. I didn't think I had. Well I was a little bit of a disappointment to him. You probably don't know, but when I was born I was one of twins. My father looked at us and said, "Oh – let's drown the ugly one". That's how I learned to swim!

However, many years ago, one very lovely Monday morning, the sun was shining and my father was sitting on the lawn. He used to spend hours on that lawn, wishing he had a house to go with it. Anyway he looked up and he thought he saw someone he knew. And he was right. It was me. He beckoned to me – he was very friendly, and he shouted "Hey ... Rover" He always wanted a dog..... He said " On our way to school.." And incidentally I should mention, he used to take me to school every morning. He had to – he was in the same class. And on our way to school he said, "I want to talk to you about your future." He said, "When you grow up, promise me you'll never ever go anywhere near a theatre. Especially the Windmill. You remember the Windmill theatre – that's where the girls used to dance round the stage barefoot – up to their

Enjoying a glass of bubbly with Pearl Carr & Teddy Johnson.

chins. He said you mustn't go – because if you do go – you'll see something you oughtn't to see." So I went. And I did see something I shouldn't have seen. FATHER! Mind you – don't misunderstand me – he was a fine man. He thought the world of his family – he never came home. And we appreciated it. Lets give him something he never had during his life …… Credit. Yes – one must be fair – he left everything he had to an orphanage. It wasn't much. Nine children. No – but there was a time in his life that he made big money. Unfortunately – it was an eighth of an inch too big. But whatever money he had he spent some on drink, some on women and the rest he spent foolishly.

Well if you remember – it's a ventriloquial act. I go off – bring on a dummy – sit it on my knee – and make it talk. Now it may seem odd – but a lot of people don't really believe I make this dummy talk. They don't believe I do it. So to prove to them that I make the dummy talk – I do allow my lips to move a little. Incidentally, I stand on one leg – like this. But then again – all ventriloquists stand on one leg – and you may have wondered why – and there is a reason. If they took the other one away - ……… now I'll go and get the dummy. I hope you do enjoy this act – but if you don't like it – don't worry. It's no good us both worrying. But sit there – watch it – and judge it for what it is. I'm not asking for sympathy – I'm begging for it.

ORCHESTRA: VENT PLAY ON MUSIC

Thank you for staying. Now this is the dummy. – This…… Now if you'll excuse me for a moment – I'll find the string. As you probably know – there's a string that works the mouth. I've often thought – wouldn't it be a funny thing if the string were to break. (FUMBLES AROUND)

H   Is the string all right…

F   (I DON'T KNOW)…..

H   It is

F   (GOOD SHOW).

H   I'm pulling it…

F   (I KNOW YOU ARE) ….

H   Would you like to sit down …

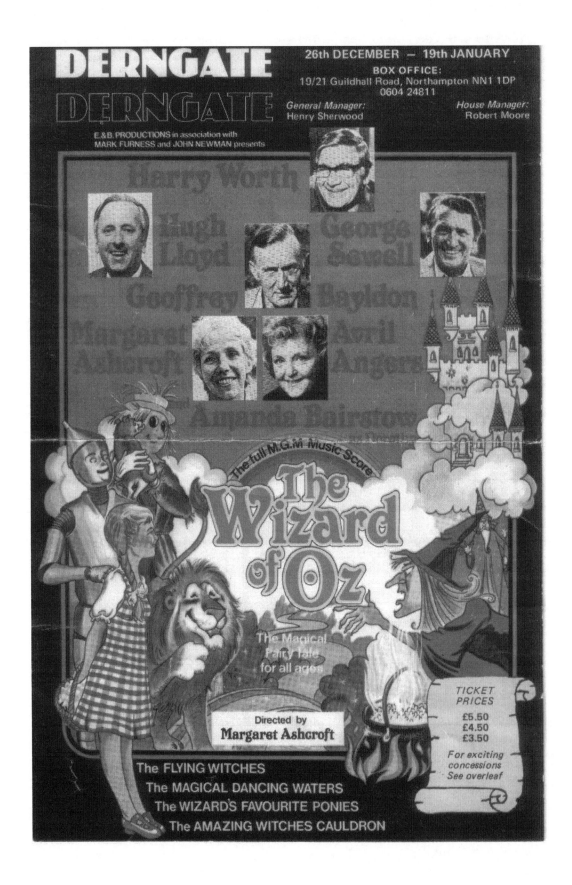

F   (THANK YOU - SQUEALS).

H   All right! Now – I beg your pardon – carry on. It's my throat …

C   (IT WANT'S CUTTING).

H   That's not a nice thing to say –

C   (NO BUT IT'S SINCERE)

This is Clarence and this is Fotheringhay.

H   Clarence – are you listening?….

C   (YERS)

H   Are you all right? …

C   (YERS)

H   Are you sure …

C   (YERS)

H   Can you do anything to entertain?

C   (I SING)

H   Ah – you sing?

C   (OH YERS)

H   Oh Clarence

C   (OH HELL)

H   Watch your language

C   (ENGLISH – WHAT'S YOURS)

H   Would you sing now?

C   (YERS)

H   Would you join in the song?

C   (IT'S RATHER EXHAUSTING)

H   Exhausting?

C   (YERS)

H   Are you ready?

C   (YERS)

H   Are you ready?

F   (YASS)

That's it – Story told. !!!

H Did he say yass?

C (YASS)

F (IS HE TAKING THE……)

H No he's not

F (I THOUGHT HE WAS)

 H No. Were you?

C (YERS)

H You were?

C (YERS)

H He was

F (I THOUGHT HE WAS)

C (WHAT ABOUT YOU?)

H Me?

C (YERS)

H I don't know if I'm coming or going.

C (YOU DON'T LOOK GOOD EITHER WAY

H Oh , I'll join in this song – but I should warn you – I'm just a ventriloquist.

C (YES YOU ARE – JUST!)

ORCHESTRA: INTO SUNNY SIDE OF THE STREET

Thank you very much. It's very kind of you. I'd love to do some more – but to tell you the truth, I don't know anymore. No – there's more to it than that. If I do more, the show runs late – I get home late. And if I get home late – my wife lets the room. But I don't know why I say these awful things about her. She really is a Miss World. Well she could be the state the worlds in. But even so – I go home every night. I'm not welcome – but it is somewhere to go. Believe me – every time I put my key in the lock and open the door I wonder what I am letting myself in for.

Well if I get home early she thinks I'm after something and if I get home late she thinks I've found it!

Nevertheless – I'm sure….

SONG: SOMEBODY LOVES ME

Printed in Great Britain
by Amazon

29288876R00042